LURE FACTOR

The 5 Essential Steps That Accelerate Trust, Increase Referability & Position Financial Professionals as a Trusted Authority in any Niche

TYLER HOFFMAN

Copyright © 2017 Tyler Hoffman

All rights reserved.

ISBN-13: 978-1542876575

ISBN-10: 1542876575

CONTENTS

PREFACE
1

STEP 1: TRUST YOUR VOICE
5

STEP 2: TRUST YOUR PURPOSE
23

STEP 3: 7 TRUST DISTINCTIONS
30

STEP 4: TRUSTED LEADER
40

STEP 5: TRUSTED PROCESS
48

BONUS CHAPTER TRUST YOUR HEALTH
65

TRUST BUILDING WORKSHEETS
86

LURE FACTOR

Preface

"My father always said, Never trust anyone whose TV is bigger than their bookshelf - so I make sure I read."
-Emilia Clarke

Sitting on the tightly woven berber carpet in front the TV, my brother and I were feverishly pulling out the real estate section from each newspaper in the stacks scattered across the living room floor. Newspapers were surrounding us waist high. The PQ News came out weekly and was the local source of news for Parksville and Qualicum Beach, two seaside communities on Vancouver Island. These papers were delivered to us the night before. They came in on limited edition Cadillac, white with a royal blue cloth top. The car spoke of class and significance. My brother and I did this activity every third Thursday of the month for a few years; it was easy money – getting paid to watch G.I. Joe and He-Man cartoons as we stuffed envelopes.

We were paid a flat rate, so we learned the value of ROI early in life. The faster we could get the real estate section pulled out and stuffed into a generic envelope, the more we made. Luckily for us, we did not have to worry about the address labels or postage. It was a simple task, and Brady and I had this routine down pat.

She was born Geraldine Lorna Metcalf on March 25, 1934, in Manitoba to a blended family of 4, she was 1 of 2 girls and wealthy they were not. As a young lady, Geraldine would get on her bicycle and go from neighbour to neighbour collecting laundry for a fee, helping to contribute to the home finances. Money would be a central theme in her life as she grew, had a family, started a career and later built a real estate empire.

Later in life, Geraldine would go onto a career with RBC, the Royal Bank of Canada and become one of their first Bank Managers and best-selling Mortgage Advisors in North Vancouver. Having her eyes set on something bigger, in the 1980's she moved to Qualicum Beach, become a Real Estate Agent with Century 21 and quickly became a leading sales producer.

This transformation spawned her familiar name of Gerry. Gerry Adair. (she married and divorced). She would form a partnership which went on to buy the Century 21 Franchise, and later she became the sole owner of a Re/Max franchise and be inducted into the Re/Max Hall of Fame for her listings and sales.

There was an extended period of time that if a stranger were driving through Qualicum Beach, they might have thought that Gerry Adair was running for local office as her real estate listing signs were everywhere. Her presence was felt from Nanoose Bay to Bowser. She was the leader. She was what many Real Estate Agents aspired to become once getting their license.

The Cadillac did not stay long. It was always on a mission. As it reversed down our driveway, the porch light illuminated the license plate. Personalised, it had GERRY A on it. Gerry was my Grandmother and observing her transform two businesses and dominate an industry for a substantial fifteen-year run is in essence what Lure Factor is about. She had it.

My promise to you is to show how to build a business, grow a practice in a way that is effortless, authentic, and selfless by giving you 5 direct steps that help you become more referable.

How did Geraldine become Gerry? How had a young girl grown up in the dust of the prairies doing the laundry of her neighbours become a top producing Real Estate Agent, alongside building a business in a Franchise model? How is it that some Advisors, Accountant or Lawyers just seem always to have a flow of business that is profitable and fun? Why do some Advisors continually need to look for new business and others have raving fans that walk new clients directly over them over? Well, that would be the purpose of what we are going to uncover here. I surmount it to something I have called the "Lure Factor".

The Lure Factor is defined as a swift combination of trust building behaviours, savvy business etiquette and aligned communication. If you are ready for a fresh approach, keep turning the pages and trust that this book will give you what you are looking for.

In this book, I use the word Advisor consistently. For the context of this book, please know that this relates to Financial Advisors, Planners, Investment Advisors, Lawyers, Accountants, Notaries, FinTechs, Brokerages, Investment Advisors, Brokers. Let's get rocking!

Step 1 Trust Your Inner Voice

"The greatest revolution of my generation is the discovery that by changing the inner attitudes of your mind, you can change the outer aspects of your life." -William James

Every day we need to step up and defy the odds because that little voice inside our head is always chattering at us, isn't it? It mostly just wants to protect you and is never in touch with the real you. The voice of the mind is a globally shared experience amongst all humans. The mind's thoughts you hear aren't unique to you, everyone has had the same thought at one point in time. That little voice that drains us and wears us down can easily be ignored once you recognise it's not even you. Taming the voice and training it to serve you is the power of the untapped skill.

Are you addicted to the habit of worrying? Perhaps you are a habitual hesitator? These are prime examples of how the mind's little voice holds us back from achieving our own greatness. What we want to hear is the voice of the champion.

There's a simple concept out there called: think – feel – act. The way we think affects the way we, feel which affects the way we act.

When we listen to our thoughts as if they were our own, emotions are triggered inside of us. Our brain recognises no difference between fear and excitement.

Physiologically the response is the same. Our heart rate goes up, palms get sweaty, maybe our face gets flushed. The difference for us how we respond to that emotion brought on by how we engage those thoughts that get broadcasted in our head. Here's the new flash: you can control the station.

Is it possible to experience two different types of emotions over the same event? Let's look at the obvious scenario of you making a presentation to a large audience. The facts are: you speaking and large audience. Now, you could infer this two ways: (1) me speaking, large audience, nervous and maybe freaking out. (2) me speaking, large audience, excited, and possibly amped up.

What's the difference? Thoughts and emotions, that's it. The same set of facts, same scenario, same person, a different response to thoughts.

To get past the thoughts created by your little voice, first recognise that this is not your thought. This is the thought of the mind, and the mind is trying to protect itself.

Once the thought is recognised, we need to fill the empty space with a new positive thought and a vision of the desirable outcome. By anchoring the new thought with a vision of what you want to see as the outcome pulls you away from the negative emotions causing stress and anxiety to emotions that help prepare you and help you stay focused.

Tony Robbins has a hack that has you make a move, like clenching your first, doing a fist pump, something to break the pattern in your physiology to shift you into a more positive peak state. Mel Robbins (no relation) introduced the concept of counting backwards from 5 to help change the thought pattern. Me, I use a technique I saw from the greatest baseball movie of all-time For the Love of the Game. In the film, Kevin Costner played the part of a pitcher, and when he was on the mound, he said to himself "clear the mechanism" when he was going down a rabbit hole of little voice activity. Whatever it is, the key is we need to be present and aware so that we can intentionally break up this pattern for ourselves. No one is going to tap you on the shoulder for this.

Another tool to help you stay focused is to remind yourself "why" you are doing this and for "who." I love this concept as it anchors you to the outcome at a higher level and assists you in carrying out your purpose.

At some point, today get into a quiet space, focus on your breathing and think about all of the times over the past week where that voice in your head judged you, questioned your performance, told you not to do something, caused you to hesitate or withdraw from a conversation or activity.

With your eyes still closed and continuing to focus on your breathing, get in touch with the language you heard, the tone you felt. Was it a genuine version of yourself telling you these things or was it the mind, just doing what the mind is meant to do: protect you from feeling pain, looking bad, not looking good, fear of being rejected.

Take a moment to recognise that these thoughts and that little voice in your head are not out to serve you in this capacity, yet have shaped many experiences in your life.

Still with your eyes closed and focusing on your breath, look past these thoughts and find the voice of the champion inside you. The champion voice needs to be called upon oddly enough, though with practice you can create the champion voice to be the dominate voice in your head.

How would the champion inside your head speak to you? What tone would you hear? How different sounding would the voice be?

Do you see that as quickly has the little voice is there, it can quickly be summoned away for the champion to take over? The voice of frustration, trying to figure things out, solution seek is a voice of perpetual mediocrity. When confronted with this voice, tell the voice to silence and call upon your champion to take to over. The champion voice is direct, strong, compelling and knows when to be silenced, like when you're trying to sleep!

When you have trust and confidence in your quest to achieve your goals and are aligned with your purpose, you will not have the continual poison of resistant energy flooding your soul that the little voice stirs inside you.

Resistant energy makes people feel lost, disengaged and checked out. Often drugs (rec or pharma) are used to replace these symptoms of depression. Other activities included watching countless hours of TV or finger flicking on social media for hours on end. These distractions lead to an ordinary unfulfilled life. An example of trusting yourself is allowing you to (effortlessly) stop work every night without having to "catch-up" on stuff from the office while at home, or staying at the office late. This is a reaction to the little voice who has enslaved you.

The "stopping of work" comes from a place of abundance. When you allow yourself to experience life, connect with family, friends, your kids, dive into your hobby or look after yourself physically, you are connecting to what you value most (or should).

The "continuing of work" into the evening is coming from a dark place of lack, or not having enough or not being enough. This action is the antithesis of creating an abundantly vibrant life. Do you find yourself not getting to do what you love? If yes, why is that you value your work so much?

By having a strong connection to your ultimate purpose and living in your values, you will experience life at a level that produces abundance upon abundance. It's how the rich get richer, and the poor get poorer. In this example, if you're the type that continually brings work home or needs to go back to the office then I will challenge you here that your life is shit. It can at least be much more fulfilling. The work will always be there. Sure, you might get it done, but then there will (always) be another 10 things to do. You could be sharing connections with your friends, learning to play the clarinet, taking those signing lessons, volunteering with Big Sisters. There is allot more to your life than the files on your desk or the latest NetFlix original series to binge off habitually.

Understanding when the little voice is holding you back and tempering it with the voice of the champion is the skill that will help you to begin trusting your inner voice more regularly. A way to accelerate this ability is to allow yourself to get into a peak state more often and visualise the outcome you're after.

Peak State

Athletes call it getting in the zone, others call it flow. It's sometimes referred to as runners high. Tony Robbins' definition of peak state is that it's the key that allows you to open your own door of high performance. To get into a peak state, you could do just about anything so long as it involves you changing your physiology that will release endorphins. Go for a run, jump rope, dance, listen to music, sing in the shower. Do whatever it takes to get into a positive state.

Your peak stage emerges from a radical alteration in normal brain function. As your attention heightens, your brain uses the intrinsic system, the faster and more efficient processing of the subconscious. Essentially, you're trading energy usually used for higher cognitive functions for heightened attention and awareness. Any brain structure that would hamper rapid-fire decision-making is literally shut off allowing this peak state to alter your performance.

Visioning

There have been tonnes of evidence on the power of visioning. The most famous example is the one about the two basketball teams. One team was told to physically do 100 free throws every day for a week. Another team to visualise the throwing 100 free throws every day for a week. Both teams practised "together" at the same time and were found to be of the same athletic calibre. Guess who did better at live free throws in the second week. The team who visualised.

How do you visualise your outcomes, or do you? The more intense you imagine the future experience, the more it becomes anchored in your nervous system as being real!

The following is an exercise that can help you get into peak state and put your visual experience into your nervous system allowing your brain to feel it as being real.

All 3 phases of this exercise need to be done with you in a peak state, so keep that music up and stay pumped. Celebrate in between each of the three sets to anchor the feeling of accomplishment and gratitude for your new clarity. I have a podcast of this whole exercise that you can download to help you get the most out of it. Just visit my website, and you'll find it under <tools>.

Get into a comfortable space and crank some tunes that give you the goosebumps, that make you want to dance when no one is looking. Settle in and feel the music with your eyes closed. Take 10 breaths in, exhale and visualise the air filling up a giant balloon. Imagine all the little things that stress you out are now filling up the balloon with each exhale. These are tasks, people, things you do not want in your life.

On the 11th and final exhale, imagine peace coming over you and with your eyes still closed see that balloon zip away to the sun and explode, no more stress in your life. Focus on the calmness, the space you can now create from and think of time that you felt loved. Who was there, what was going on? What was said, can you smell or taste anything? What about touch? How does this feel? Are you smiling? Imagine having this type of love every day. Take a moment just to feel the grace of being able to experience this love right now at this moment, and forever.

Now answer this: what are three of the most important things for your life that you must have? Family, your spouse? Kids, dog, a charity? By changing your own pattern of thought and getting connected to yourself through the simple power of breath and visioning, your brain instantly became attached to this energy, didn't it? Recognise this. In a moment, you can connect with the most important things in your life.

In my workshops and webinars, we spend a whole day expanding your vision, aligning your purpose and identifying what specific negative self-talk holds you back. In this chapter, my intention is proving to you that you have the power to connect with what's important by following a programmed series of actions.

The next step is to see where you have been inauthentic with these 3 most important things in your life. Maybe you have not spent time with family because you felt the emotion of needing to work late. Perhaps it was taking your laptop on that family vacation, or you have the nasty habit of always checking your phone and not being present. What has been the impact been on them and you? Write it down right now. Get real. Look deep and get honest with yourself. Is your thought or belief 100% accurate with certainty? Can you honestly say yes when you ask yourself that? Likely the answer is no, and so what is then possible for you knowing that you've diluted your experience?

The impact of working late has meant that I don't get to read bedtime stories to my son and I don't feel as connected to him and often feel guilty for working so much.

Once the intensity has been discovered, and you see it for what it truly is, an illusion, there is an empty space that opens up for you to create a new possibility. What will that be for you? In this example, maybe it looks like this:

The possibility I have for my son is the possibility of us having entertaining reading time that we create compelling characters and discover new worlds.

Be bold and creative with your vivid use of language. Wouldn't you agree that the above is much better than:

The possibility I have for my son is the possibility of me reading to him the very night.

The more vivid your language, the more vibrant your experience. I still remember stories my Granny (Dad's mom) told us as kids because she creates an imaginary world that opened adventure and intrigue. Carry this vividly delicious language over into all your action planning.

The next step is to acknowledge your inauthenticity with whoever it is and declaring what is now possible for both of you. It's harder because you need to be vulnerable and show intimacy. Cast a wider view and look out into your world of where you are out of integrity with people. You can restore it today with them, and need to restore it with them to be trusted. Use the same process as above. To get the full effect of the lure factor, you need to be whole, to yourself and others.

Negative Thought Conversion

You can use the same formula above and apply it to all aspects of your business. There are areas right now that you doubt about yourself. You have agreements that you operate by regarding the peer groups that you have chosen to run with. All of which supports any limited view you have of yourself and the opportunity in front of you.

Here are a few that seem to resonate often for professionals:

- *I don't have a big enough network*
- *My prospects don't have enough money*
- *My admin/sales team is too Jr.*
- *Our firm doesn't have the resources*
- *Our products aren't competitive*
- *The regulators are making it too hard to prospect*
- *Compliance will never approve that*

Take 10 minutes and identify areas that have self-doubt, frustration, lack of confidence, areas that you are procrastinating around. Get them all out on paper.

Once you are encountered with this doubt, your energy is routed to synapses in your brain firing off the message "this won't work." So, you either ditch the prospects of fulfilling the idea or just settle for what you have now and continue to be frustrated. Sometimes you may even take it a step further and find peer groups that support your beliefs. By doing this, you will always be "right" and have support with your wallowing. It's what humans do well. This pattern can be broken, and this is how you can do it.

The next time you have encountered such negative self-talk going on in your brain snap your fingers in front of your eyes. Seriously, the change in your physiology will literally snap you out of it allowing you to reframe your thoughts. You could do anything really, but likely it's better than shaking your ass, although that could be fun.

Once you're snapped out of it, understand that you reached that negativity because you were not resourceful enough. Many times we may feel that we need more tools, resources, skills, people, money or time to get the job done or achieve the outcome. You don't require more resources to achieve what you want and need. Instead, consider you need to be more resourceful. Play a bigger game with higher standards for yourself and add more accountability. Own your thoughts, and you will own your experiences.

Using the same list above here are how you could reproach those feelings of "not having" or "not being enough."

- *I don't have a big enough network*
    - *I love that I can grow my network*
- *My prospects don't have enough money*
    - *It's exciting to know there are wealthy prospects available to me*
- *My admin/sales team is too Jr.*
    - *My leadership can influence the direction of my team*
- *Our firm doesn't have the resources*
    - *I am a thought leader and can cultivate what I need to achieve*
- *Our products aren't competitive*
    - *By serving a niche market, our products can help many people*
- *The regulators are making it too hard to prospect*
    - *There is a continual source of candidates that need to meet me*
- *Compliance will never approve that*
    - *They just might not! So, find something they will approve and get off it!*

The answers and activities are there for you, it just requires a 2mm shift in your mindset. It's the smallest of changes that often reward us with the largest of payoffs.

Taking it another step further you could now easily identify some action items to help you advance in areas that you were previously holding yourself back in.

- *I don't have a big enough network*
    - *I love that I can grow my network*
        - *Explore networking opportunities in my city*
        - *Find someone who has an extensive network and take them for lunch*

- *My prospects don't have enough money*
    - *It's exciting to know there are wealthy prospects available to me*
        - *Write down 5 reasons why wealthy people will deal with me*
        - *Make a list of my top 5 clients and take them for lunch*

- *My admin/sales team is too Jr.*
    - *My leadership can influence the direction of my team*
        - *Look for training courses specific to our needs*
        - *Find a freelancer who can compliment our team*

- *Our firm doesn't have the resources*
  - *I am a thought leader and can cultivate what I need to achieve*
    - *Make a list of what I need and why present to "boss."*
    - *Source other firms that have what I need to serve my client's better*

- *Our products aren't competitive*
  - *By serving a niche market, our products can help many people*
    - *Which demographics are our products competitive in?*
    - *Align my marketing with this niche demographic*

- *The regulators are making it too hard to prospect*
  - *There is a continual source of prospects that need to meet me*
    - *Identify 3 new networking groups*
    - *Where could I volunteer?*

- *Compliance will never approve that*
  - *They just might not! So, find something they will approve and get off it!*

Self Suffering

What about being inauthentic with yourself? Did that come up at all for you in this exercise? Do you suffer over yourself? By buying this book, you're likely an Achiever and Achievers generally have the perfectionist complex. It comes from the world of lack, not being good enough, not having enough. These feeling are overcompensated by always on the quest for getting it perfectly right or continually improving.

Maybe you need to forgive yourself for being too critical of you. Where have you been constantly frustrated? Are there things you are not doing or being, that you think about all the time. Anything you're just tired of? What do you say to yourself when things don't go your way? Stupid idiot? Told you so? I'm weak? I wasn't going make it anyway?

What have you been telling yourself all these years that is just a bunch of bullshit? Do you want to continue to suffer over not being good enough, not having enough, feeling like you're never going to become who were meant to be? It's all just story you told yourself anyway, and it's not even real. You have taken an event that happened to you as a child, added your own meaning and now everything you do or don't do is tied to reinforcing that story you have created for yourself and lived your life by.

A 4-year-old is running the direction of your life, and you likely didn't even know. Time to lay that little bastard off and put yourself back in control.

That's a sad existence, though, isn't it? You can change it right now by recognising that's not even your voice talking to you. Your authentic voice is a warrior, a champion and what would a champion say to you? Would a champion suffer? Go ahead and revisit the above exercise and look at yourself.

Some serious data is being generated in neuroscience. Our brains can be rewired, reprogrammed and what I like to refer to as being reconditioned. This process is a deliberate way of shifting your mind. It's that 2mm shift. If you do this enough times, you can recondition your mind to immediately go to the positive side of the challenge and create a solution much more readily. Making this thinking automatic is where Gerry got to all the time. She was rarely ever in doubt. If Gerry faced an obstacle, she immediately went into solution source mode. Family needed money has a kid, she got on a bike and collected laundry.

There was a time that Gerry had to get custody of one of her grandchildren. For most of us, this would slightly derail us. Gerry dug in, hired the right people, marketing more efficiently through this time and trusted her admin team to get the job done. She came out on the other side stronger than when she went into it. Was it easy? No. Was she under stress? Yes. Did she quit, falter, give in, surrender. Heck no. She got up every day like she had every other day and set a new standard for herself. She defied the odds and battled to get what was important to her.

We need to fight for what we want every day. Each morning we need to rise and cast away the fear and self-conscious talk that shackles us from reaching our dreams. We must be a gladiator every day and search for the voice of the champion.

Step 2: Expand Your Uniqueness to Live Your Purpose

"Most of us have two lives: the life we live and the unlived life within us. Between the two stands resistance."
-Steven Press

What is your why? Why did you get into the business you're in? Why do you want to do this work? Who is your practice serving and what is the ultimate impact for those you serve?

If you were to go the web pages of most Accountants, Advisors, wealth management firms, you would see the same website done the same way. Products, Services, About the Team and Contact us. I am going to let you in on a little secret: no one gives a shit what you sell. The fact that you do tax planning or offer no-fee accounts means nothing from a marketing perspective. Websites like this only help to further commoditize an industry already lacking in emotional innovation.

Honestly, do you think that by saying you serve high net worth families save tax, is really going to attract people to you? What if your website's sole message was a soul message: *We create the possibility of parents creating access to higher education for their children so that their legacy withstands time and has a sense of honour.* Just a quick example of how you can make a small shift to get significant gains by focusing on what your purpose is and communicating it in a delicious way.

For many professionals, they know the business they are in but are unaware of the business that they are really in. For instance, I could easily say that I am a Business Consultant for Financial Professionals. That's the business I am in, but the business I am really in is: optimising trust for professionals, so their practice can thrive in a down economy, removing stress at home; and prosperously expand beyond what they thought possible allowing their family to live a great life.

This central theme reoccurs in all my marketing. My clients and relatives know precisely what I stand for and why I do what I do. Like many of us, I grew up in a household where for many years money was a stressor. I knew at a very early age that this was not going to be something I would have in my adult life and I don't. Now I create the possibility of helping others have abundance.

Who are You Really?

What about you? Why do you get up every morning and charge on? What's your mission? Do your clients know? How are you communicating your why? Are you living your why?

Aligning with your purpose should be easy, but often our small voice shuts down the creativity and drive, for fear of failure, looking bad or feeling like we aren't good enough for "that."

Are you doing what you want to do or do you feel stale, stagnant and bored? If money were no object would you still be doing what you are right now?

Consider taking 1 hour a week to work on connecting to your vision and purpose.

A) Connect to your inner drive

- What's your dream vision?
- What's your actual purpose?
- Who are you really?
- What values do you live by?
- What passions do you want to explore?

B) What outcomes do you desire?

- Business
- Personal
- Community
- Spiritual
- Wellbeing

C) What actions are needed to get the outcome?

- Brainstorm, mastermind, mentorship?
- What resources are required?
- What can you do to be more resourceful?

D) Schedule what must get done

- Time block
- Know why you must get these outcomes

E) Identify possible challenges and outline how you will respond?

- Look down the road ahead to see potential hazards or roadblocks.

It's easy to get caught up into the 9 to 5 of a business and the routine of going home. Life is meant to be extraordinary. Humans are the happiest when we are experiencing progress or contributing to others. By taking 1 hour a week to connect with what drives your soul, blocking time and assigning resources, will allow you to have a deeper sense of purpose with all those you have relationships with and life a life of joy.

This process also allows you to add a tremendous sense of value to your clients, as this process can be shared with them and help them design their dream life too. By having a private exchange of each other's values, visions, and purpose you begin to become the trusted Advisor.

What if you added a dimension of this exercise to your client annual review meeting? How would that impact the relationships you have, and what sort of transformation might occur for your clients with you being the source of it all?

It's about raising your standards. Craving a higher standard of life or business requires having the standard of connecting with your purpose habitually without defaulting because of some lame-ass excuse that means nothing. Try it for 30 days and see how good you feel and how much fun living really is.

Alter Ego

However, perhaps to operate at this level, the real version of yourself, you need to tap into your alter ego, a persona, a modified identity? Having access to this version of you is a way to help you get into peak state, capture the confidence and articulation of the superhero you. Your inner Rockstar.

Think about all the different relationships you have: Advisor, team leader, father, mother, sister, teammate, friend, husband, wife. Isn't it already true that for each of those relationships you mute part of your personality and amp up others?

If you've ever had children, you know that they need you to show up as playful, patient and understanding. In sports, as a teammate, you need to be competitive, strategic and collaborative. Turn Up that way with your kids and resentment is going to divide you. Arrive on the court being playful and patient and you will sure to be benched quickly.

Do you ever feel that there is a stronger, more confident version of you somewhere inside you? If you could tap into that energy every occasionally, what would it do for you?

Looking at the iconic alter ego relationship between Clark Kent and Superman, who would you say is who? Was Superman the truest version of himself or was Clark? Clark was the muted, tamed version of the real person. He had to adjust his personality to fit in, be accepted and operate in a world that wasn't ready for who he really was: a superhero.

Are there a Superman or Wonder Woman inside of you? If yes, how do you let them out and influence your ability to achieve success, live fully, tap into your purpose? This isn't about having a split personality or being inauthentic. It's about getting into peak state to achieve the outcome and feel the experience in whole.

Richard, an executive, carries a small polished rock in his pocket from his grandparent's farm. They immigrated to Canada to create a better life for their nine kids. This rock reminds him that anything is possible with hard work. Janette has a bracelet that her mom gave her when she was battling breast cancer and won the fight. This real wonder woman has a constant reminder on her wrist every day that she can win. Music can also work, Ed listens to "Eye of the Tiger" before going into every major negotiation to get him front and centre with his inner Rocky so he stay's focussed on the outcome. Gerry Adair had her Cadillac and Nana Mouskouri playing in the car stereo to help her tap into Gerry. Geraldine was long forgotten.

To help to craft your alter ego, think about times when you felt unstoppable, what happened for you to feel that way? What preparation did you take to get the win? The emotions you felt, what were they? List them on a piece of paper right now, along with your physiology at the time. Were you standing? How were you standing? Did you celebrate? How? Visually recreate this event and flood yourself with everything you experienced at the time.

Now, name this version you. Lay claim this Rockstar inside of you. If you took this version of you into the client meeting, board room, or negotiation what would be the effect? Could you get shit done? Would other's follow your confident lead more often?

Fulfilling your purpose and living out your mission is a gift that we all have resting inside of us. Your mission, when carried out to its' full potential will impact thousands, if not; millions of people. By getting clear on your values, knowing precisely how you want to feel and tapping your inner Clark Kent to take a break once in a while, will make it all the more fun and achievable.

Step 3: Put The 7 Distinctions of Trust in Motion

"As soon as you trust yourself, you will know how to live."
-Johann Wolfgang von Goethe

You could ask 100 people what their definition of trust is and likely get about 100 different views. Trust is an abstract concept, much like love. Your values and belief systems help you form the construct of trust. You use the past to filter the future, making trust very personal.

There are some common elements and models that you can use to help yourself navigate the all-important territory of trust. The easiest model to understand is the model presented by Michelle and Dennis Reina in their book Trust & Betrayal in the Workplace. It's an easy straight forward read packed with years of reliable research and compelling data that you can put to work right away. They have built a Trust Consulting Practice that has a global reach which some of the biggest names in business.

Their model focuses on the three C's: Character, Capabilities and Communication. This chapter will include an examination of those three, plus four more of my own: Confidence, Charisma, Collaboration and Capacity.

Often when you think of trust, reliability, being honest, showing up on time and getting the job done are often what you might first think of. The belief is for many of us that if you do these activities, you earn trust. A + B = C. It doesn't work like that. However, there is an actual trust building equation. In his book *The Trusted Advisor*, Charles Green introduced the trust quotient as being:

$$C + R + I / \text{Self-Orientation} = \text{Trustworthiness}$$

$$C = \text{credibility}, R = \text{reliability}, I = \text{intimacy}$$

On the surface, these are transactional elements. Together they begin to form the matrix we know as trust. Done consistently through continuous never ending improvement, trust can be accelerated.

The analogy of Trust being a bicycle is an excellent way to illustrate this. A wheel has many spokes on it to help keep the wheel's shape when it's performing. Otherwise, it would collapse. If we consider the spokes being replaced by each of those C's we can begin to understand the relationship and dependence they each have on the other. Without one there is none.

Let's look at each of them.

Character: managing expectations, keeping your word and agreements, establishing and respecting boundaries, delegating appropriately and creating win-win relationships.

A person with a high score of trust in character will find themselves clarifying the objectives for others. They remove the grey and help to construct the world that everyone knows the rules of the game so that everyone has a chance to win. They won't delegate just to shift work. Instead, they delegate to strengths, create an opportunity for others, gain a new perspective, and they do so by inviting others into a possibility rather than a project or task. The outcome for both is evident.

Capabilities: having confidence in your competence, your team's skills, ability to manage demands and expectations placed on you.

Your clients will see and feel this in action, by how you respond, jump into conversations and pivot when challenged. They most often though will also be exposed to your team and how they deliver or don't provide your high-touch customer service.

For a trusted Advisor having the designations of higher education and certifications will lend itself to creating trust around your capabilities and skills. In the "giver's gain" philosophy you would be best served to acknowledge the abilities of others.

This authentic exchange shows what you value, but also creates a sense of intimacy. A pitfall where this could break down is when you are in the process of learning a new skill or presenting a new product or service.

Trust is going to come from your ability to articulate the value you are offering and having the data to back it up. In a team environment, adopting the mantra that "everybody gets it" ensures that your leadership stands for cohesive understanding and that "no man is left behind" in the learning process.

Communication: admitting to mistakes, not gossiping, edifying others, maintaining confidentiality, telling the truth, giving and taking constructive feedback, and speaking with a purpose.

Scoring high in trust of communication will have you being a person that shifts conversations when others start talking about people behind their back. When you introduce others, you do it in a way that elevates them to a stage as opposed to just announcing their name.

It might look like this. Hi team, this Tyler Hoffman, he is a Trust Coach that helps Advisors accelerate trust inside their practice. As opposed to, this is Tyler Hoffman, he's a Business Coach. Individuals that score high in communication also have no problem with humility, they can admit (even to themselves) when things went sideways.

James, a Partner in a law firm, had a team of Assistants that loved to get together in the lunch room and talk about the latest problem client. They would use this entertainment regularly, and the habit became so bad that one day James walked in with one these "problem clients" to fill up their coffee cups. [Insert awkward moment here] This negative energy serves no one. It undermines the client, and that energy is transferred. It shows up in the tone of the emails, promptness of the replies and high not a high functioning skill of a dynamic team.

Charisma: engaging others through authenticity, presenting possibilities, responding quickly with a positive tone, having a quiet confidence with a strong sense of determined confidence.

Often thought of as an innate trait, like these 7 C's charisma can be learned. Charismatic individuals have a global view that often goes against the status quo, they seek alternative routes and can speak intelligently with passion and create a vision for others to follow. They generally make quick and accurate decisions.

Collaboration: seeking to understand others, including others, respecting viewpoints, listening with purpose, involving others in the process.

An active collaborator cultivates trust by asking fantastic questions and looks to bring others into the process. Advisors can raise their trust score by having their clients and prospects be part of the actual proposal building. Trusted Advisors will seek the client's input in person as they are creating the strategy.

Most Advisors don't do this because they operate from a place of lack. "It will take too much time," "they will feel the process takes too long," etc. The reality is by having your clients and prospect be part of this bespoke process they will believe your ideas more and have a connection to the results because they were a part of the process. This alone is an easy way to differentiate yourself and get the luring factor working vigorously for you.

Patricia, a Financial Planner, used to always meet with her prospects, collect the data and come back a week later to present the data and "sell the plan." Until one time she had a prospect ask to work on the proposal together. Reluctant, she said yes not sure of what to expect. What she found was that by having the prospect be part of the process, she could develop the relationship much deeper, and quicker.

She could ask more questions, create further clarity on what the prospect wanted and who he was and was not. Certain scenarios could be explored first without wasting time later. In the end, she only put in an extra 3 or four hours but earned the client without having to "land" him because they arrived at a conclusion together. Because he was a part of the process the confidence, trust in capabilities, trust in communication, were all there.

Confidence: having your beliefs and values aligned with your purpose, communication with unwavering intent, removing ambiguity, understanding silence.

Scoring high in confidence means you clearly know why you are heading where you are going. You know your values, and have activities that support you in the quest of the end goal. You remove ambiguity because you do your homework, have thought about what that means to others and can speak to it because you know the data or know precisely where it could be found. You use silence to highlight your point view and allow the space for others to think. You are not a steam roller spewing facts that make you or your film look good. Instead, you articulate everything from their point of view because you know it will benefit them.

Confidence is not about your ego, it is about knowing what you are presenting or sharing is truly in the best interest of your clients and prospects.

Capacity: knowing the limit of where resources are at, being clear when to say no, the ability to analyse quickly with accuracy, having political awareness.

Scoring low in capacity would have you agreeing to something and not being able to deliver it because you were unaware of how much time, money or people would be needed to complete it. Scoring low would have you passing on a project to a team or colleague with a predetermined deadline without collaborating with them first. Scoring high, you have the political awareness of how the commitment will impact others.

These 7 Cs are interpersonal reactions that either adds to (or takes away from) your trust bank your clients have with you. The trust bank is fueled by how much or how little oxytocin they receive from these types of interactions.

The endorphins created in a peak state allow us to perform better, make better, more accurately authentic relationships.

Therefore, it's critical that you get into a peak state heading into client meetings and presentations. Music, motivational speeches, or giving yourself a quick pep-talk in a mirror will help you get there. Getting these endorphins working for you is wonderful. Getting them to work for your clients and prospects will be transformational for your business.

The amount of oxytocin that you help create in your clients and prospects brain will determine if they work with you, promote you to their friends and get on your bandwagon. Oxytocin will specifically affect your clients and prospects willingness to accept social risks (hiring you and going with your plan) arising through interpersonal interactions.

Amsterdam scientists Shaul Shalvia and Carsten De Dreub tested the effects of oxytocin in an experimental game set up that allowed participants to lie to benefit the group. Players sniffed either a placebo or oxytocin, then played a game where teams of three anonymous participants were asked to predict a virtual coin toss.

Afterwards, they were told to report whether they had guessed correctly, with correct guessing resulting in more cash for everyone. All the participants cheated, saying that they guessed right more than they really did, but those that huffed the so-called moral molecule lied more and more quickly, saying they were right a statistically-impossible 80% of the time.

However, when the experiment was repeated, and the participants were told that only their own earnings would be increased, the oxytocin-smellers stopped lying more than the control group (though all of them still lied a little).

When correct answers had no gains or resulted in lost money, the love drug group also didn't differ from the placebo-sniffers. These results suggested that oxytocin only increased dishonesty when it strongly benefitted the group.

Oxytocin is primarily a molecule of social connection. It affects every aspect of your social and economic life, from who you choose to make investment decisions on your behalf to how much money you donate to charity. Oxytocin tells your brain when to trust and when to remain wary, when to give and when to hold back.

Conceptually, every action or inaction either pays a dividend or collects a tax. The more dividends being generated, the higher level of oxytocin being created by your client over the relationship they have with you. A question to ask yourself is: "in what I'm doing, does it move, touch and inspire my audience?"

This high standard of intimacy also has a close relationship with your level of emotional intelligence and observational awareness. Being able to pick up on tone, social cues, body language and personality style is essential for the Advisor wanting to enhance their Lure Factor.

Emotional intelligence is defined in several ways and includes the ability to understand, perceive, and use emotions to enhance thought and relationships. Preliminary research indicates that emotional intelligence and trust are related to each other.

By knowing the impact and effects of each of the 7 dimensions of trust on how they can chemically affect us and those we serve, a trusted advisor then has super powers at their disposal. Trust is gained incrementally over time through positive reinforcement and continuous repetition.

Step 4: Become a Trusted Leader to Rock Your Niche

"The key to successful leadership today is influence, not authority." -Ken Blanchard

To become a leader in your market, you need to control the messaging to your audience, and be consistent with that message and continually add massive amounts of value to them. By following these simple principles, you can serve any niche you desire. As long as you understand the pain points of that niche and communicate in a heartfelt way, the notion of positioning yourself as a trusted leader for them is very possible.

It's important to know that all human beings have the following needs regardless of culture, background or socio-economic status:

1. Certainty/Comfort
2. Uncertainty/Variety
3. Significance
4. Love/Connection
5. Growth
6. Contribution

When you align your marketing and servicing to these six needs, your prospects and clients will extend trust further and faster to you.

Imagine if your proposal hit all six. If you incorporated

these themes into your conversations how connected do you think your clients would feel? A Trusted Advisor masters focussing on these six needs in each client conversation versus spending too much time explaining the products and uncovering features and benefits in singular form. Most clients would rather talk about what's important to them, not how you do your job, so everything needs to be linked back to them following the 6 human needs.

To become a trusted leader and have the ability to influence others to take action, you need credibility. Understanding how and when to tap into the six human needs will help you accelerate trust and show that you are intelligent, but you also need a stage to broadcast from.

You might be thinking, "Right now I don't have the credibility" or "I don't know enough about that market" or "will they take me seriously?" These limiting beliefs will only be true if you own them as fact. If you're currently experiencing a roller coaster effect of clients and cash flow, you likely have one or more of these limiting belief at play this moment.

By leveraging existing content and the expertise of thought leaders, you can immediately position yourself as a trusted source for your community. You don't have to be cranking out original content every waking hour and hoping that people respond to you. This hope and pray method offers no certainty.

First, you need to know who your market is. Specifically, you need to know the following about your market: what are are your prospect's goals and what does your audience want to accomplish? What are your prospect's challenges and pain points that they need a solution for? Where do they hang out (what do they read, what social media platform are they on, what groups do they join, what conferences does your market attend, etc.) and finally, what will you future client's objections be in doing business with you? What risks can you eliminate for them to make it easier to do business with you?

Secondly, you need to build your trusted platform. There are two key steps for this. Ultimately you want to be the leader of your own group, the founder of a community. This can be built for free on either Facebook or LinkedIn. However, before jumping online and creating your group, you need to build credibility and research your market's pain points and challenges.

Find three to five groups to join on either LinkedIn or Facebook, and become an active participant by adding value and NOT promoting yourself. Listen for trends and watch for patterns within each group. This intelligence will allow you to better serve your future audience. Pay attention to the hosts of those groups and see what they do well and what they could improve on so that you can take the best practices to your new group.

A big tip here to help you optimise your presence on LinkedIn. Where possible, without upsetting your firm's compliance department or the regulators, ditch your job title. Instead, consider enhancing your professional headline. Many people use that headline spot to put in their title. The headline can pull people to you. Have you ever gone to a networking event and someone asked you're the question: "what you do?" and you said with pride: "I'm an Accountant." The conversation pretty much died, because how sexy is accounting? Instead, our job title should show up in the true form where compliance and regulations say it must. Outside that, we have free range to be creative.

So I present to you today that your job title should not be Financial Advisor, Accountant or Mortgage Broker for example. In LinkedIn, you have the capacity to have a "professional headline." This space allows you to be creative and stand out from the rest within your profession. Instead of putting "Financial Advisor" in the headline, you can put your slogan or motto. A few examples are: "Destressing Family Finances," "Uncovering Hidden Wealth," or "Protecting Solopreneurs." Use juicy imaginative language that pulls people into your sphere, allowing you to deliberately lure those you serve. This will help your ideal market notice and align with you very quickly.

The group you eventually create and manage needs to built for your audience. You are simply the host at the party cultivating conversations, adding value and providing timely information to the niche you serve.

The name of your group needs to be strategically attractive as well. If you are a Mortgage Broker the name of your group shouldn't be: Vancouver Home Owners, or Condo Financing. Instead, it could be: Vancouver Heritage Homes Community or Trusted Condo Living Strategies. You get the idea.

To accelerate your position as a Trusted Advisor in your new group, here are a few best practices to deploy when you launch:

Personal Invitation

From your other groups that you used for market research, you likely will identify key professionals you would like to have as a member of your own community. Reach out to them on the basis that you'd like them to consider joining your professional network as you are the Founder of Vancouver Heritage Homes Community and you felt they could benefit and contribute to the online group.

Welcome Message

Once they join the group, send a welcome message as

opposed to a thank you message. A welcome message is for them, their new group, whereas a thank you message conveys the tone of thanking them for joining your group. It's subtle, but greatness is in the nuances. LinkedIn has a built-in feature that can handle this for you automatically.

Phone Connection

Offer to connect with your new member over a quick phone call to learn more about what they are looking for out of the group. Use this conversation to establish rapport, gather ideas. Don't bring up your business unless they ask more about it.

Guest Appearances

Bring in guests that will be able to add value to the group. This can be especially effective when individual events are happening, like elections, market conditions, home assessments, tax time deadlines, etc.

Email Letters

Have a 3-5 email letter drip campaign that goes out to them personally (not mail chimp or other email programs) directly from you. Every 2 weeks they get an email message, that offers something that will help them. At the end of this you then will follow-up (phone is best) using this script: "Hi Tom, it's Tyler Hoffman from the Vancouver Heritage House Community. What's the best thing you've liked about what I have been sending you the last little while? Excellent! That's exactly why I wanted to connect with you today. If I could help you with that, would it make sense for us to connect in person to learn how?" Worst case scenario is we get to meet in the real world, and you get a free cup of coffee. How does next Tuesday or Thursday sound?"

These same principles can be used to gain media contacts, speaking engagements and getting invited on podcasts. Go to Association websites that align with your market and invite each of the board of directors to your group. Maybe there is a news reporter or a journalist that you could connect with. You can also develop a group of referral partners or centre of influences using this same method. It's all about concentrated effort, time blocking to achieve your outcomes and following the process over and over again.

Becoming a leader to rock the niche you serve is achievable by doing a little bit of consistent activity each day and by adding a tremendous amount of value to your audience. By cultivating a group and systematically delivering quality content that keeps you top of mind and connecting with them one on one, will give you the edge to sustain your practice.

If you don't have a niche use the worksheet in the back of the book to help you zero in on a market. Before heading to the next chapter, let me introduce you to an Advisor by the name of Ray.

Ray loves to golf. He lives in Arizona and has a financial planning practice, which caters to business owners. However, these aren't just any business owners, they are owners of golf courses. He has partnered up with a Lawyer, and an Accountant and the three of them serve a broad audience of Golf Courses, they also get to golf a lot for free!

Serving a niche requires having the voice of a champion and the belief that this laser-like focus will bring abundance. The velocity at which your practice grows is at the rate at which your audience sees you as an authoritative expert.

So if Ray was to come at it from the viewpoint of: "What about all of the other prospects I meet that aren't connected to golf? Won't I lose out on business?" This it the little voice again. The answer to this is really a question: do you want to accelerate your growth in a targeted audience or be seen as just another Advisor?

Step 5: Deliberately Add Trust to Your Processes

"It is essential to employ, trust, and reward those whose perspective, ability and judgment are radically different from yours. It is also rare, for it requires uncommon humility, tolerance, and wisdom."-Dee Hock

Take a few moments to reflect on the type of experience you want your prospects and clients to feel overall. Professional? Casual? Confident? Relatable? Polished? Organic? Staunchy? Relaxed? High energy? Edgy? Nurturing?

Whatever it is, that feeling needs to show up in each and every phase of your practice. From prospecting to pitching to onboarding to servicing. Consistency is key. There is another emotion that a Trusted Advisor is also excellent at delivering and that is empathy. Most often easier for women to provide then men, but empathy bridges the relationship and provides a level of intimacy needed for high-trust.

According to the dictionary, **empathy** is *"the intellectual identification with or vicarious experiencing of the feelings, thoughts, or attitudes of another."*

We are said to have empathy for another person when we understand what they're feeling and what they're thinking. Our empathy allows us to understand how people perceive things, how they feel, and what we can do to help them be at their best.

Trust in Marketing

Your marketing needs to be authentic, real and timely. Using stock photography like the silver-haired couple running on the beach in white linen doesn't construe trust, nor creativity. Use real photos of yourself, your team and clients to convey the connected message this is us, and we are here to serve you. Spend the money! Hire a professional photographer to take amazing pictures of you, the ROI generated in priceless!

Timely marketing is necessary as it shows how thoughtful you are. If you are perceived as someone who takes lots of care and attention to timely marketing, you will collect trust dividends, the more you collect, the more trustworthy you are believed to be. A perfect example is this bus ad that was seen in Vancouver, BC. It was a reputable Realtor who had taken out an ad on the back of a bus, which is common. But in this case, the ad was saying Happy Holiday's, and it was mid-February. Why was the ad still running? If the Realtor can't think that through maybe he can't think through a negotiation or contract? What perception is given off in this scenario? Being timely is essential. We want to be seen as clever, not careless.

Social media is the ultimate form of leverage in your marketing. But with any leveraging strategy both the gains and losses are amplified. I have seen many professionals thrive on social media and others dig their grave on a daily basis, almost always unknowingly. Here are three immediate ways social media will kill your trust.

#1 Political Views

In sales 101 you were likely told to never talk about sex, religion or politics with your clients. The same goes for social media. Free speech and standing up for causes you believe in are important. Just know that you are on display in social media. In the USA politics is much more divisive than it is in Canada but still, your views will not align with some of your followers, and that may slow down your growth and impact your ability to be referrable. Having separate accounts for personal and business makes sense, as you can direct your message and filter your actions. Think twice about your next Trump post or Oil Pipeline comment, as many don't share your views.

#2 Liking & Following

Isagenix is a performance nutrition company, they don't pay for athlete endorsements, nor do they seek them out, yet the company has many. That integrity is easy to get behind. Within your social media feeds everything you like and follow is an endorsement. Is says something about what you stand for, get behind, like and have an interest towards. The regulators don't like this either, check your state or provincial authorities stance on this as it could b perceived as an endorsement from you.

Be deliberate and intentional on who/what you like and or follow, it might just make the difference of growing your community of engaged clients. It's all about the energy you create, and the message you send with each action.

#3 Crab Traps

In the coastal waters of BC, all it takes to catch crabs is a can of tuna and a trap on the end of the 20-foot rope. Of course, you empty the can into to the trap in case you were wondering. These land mines are littered on Facebook too. "I just saved a client $1,500 in taxes, I love my job!" This style of posting is a social media crab trap. The poster is hoping to snare some interest. It's a sleazy backhanded approach. Instead, why not have your client post (and tag you in it): "So happy, our ADVISOR just saved us $1,500 in taxes – loved his process too!" Isn't that what you really want?

Client Meetings

How you deliver your client meetings and subsequent interactions all lend itself to how referrable you are. Your "referability" is your "Lure Factor." You either collect trust dividends and grow or pay trust tax and flounder in frustration and client apathy.

The First Interview

The first meeting appointment confirmation:

First impressions are everything and how you set the tone can immediately start adding dividends to your trust bank with the new prospect. You NEED to have a high touch "press kit." Preferably a custom brochure, letter, business card, hand written note in a beautiful folder. We are now seeing video folders that present an HD video. These are pricey, especially if you add in courier costs but the impression you make is first class.

Your press kit needs to focus on your purpose, passions, vision for your clients, your why and NOT your products and services. A little bit of your process in the form of a graphic will be ok. Social proof is important too, so using client testimonials with their picture or video will further connect you.

The outcome is for you to create an emotional connection. Use pictures of you professionally and casually, have your family your dog your other clients in it as well as any members of your team. Most importantly state your promise. Keep in mind you also want this to resonate with their needs and convey the overall feel you are looking to consistently broadcast.

Most people align with safety, security, privacy, and controlled growth. Family, community and empathy are the others. People care more about the idea that you care and not by how much you know or how diversified your product shelf is.

In your email appointment confirmation, aside from confirming the date and time, I suggest you make it easier for your prospect to find you. Be helpful and kind. Include a map with the cross street, where parking is located. Is there construction going on in the area? Is traffic is bad at a particular time, etc.? It's these small things that pay dividends for you. A short video clip also works well, an easy way to make a little introduction too.

If you need to them to bring or complete anything prior, sending a checklist will help them get organised. Keep it branded and add emotion to it. Perhaps it's your favourite quote. Remember the question: "is what I am doing going to move, touch and inspire my audience?" Essentially, it's about adding value.

The reminder:

Two days before the meeting a reminder text is ideal, as opposed to a generic email. Send them a personalised, quick video reminding of the date and time and that you are looking forward to meeting them. The personalised approach creates a ka-ching in your trust bank, and you can be sure they received it.

The interview:

The meeting/presentation is for them not you. It needs to

align with their needs that I mentioned earlier (safety, security, privacy, preservation of capital, family, community, empathy) and controlled growth. To get more ka-chings happening for you, you need to create that emotional element in all that you do, while remaining professional and finding ways to highlight why you are the best Advisor for them. By sharing your vision and connecting the goals of your clients back to how you can support them is the art of the first interview. It also demonstrates a high level of national intelligence. To elevate this, you can do so by asking great questions.

A strong differentiator is to ask questions that are so amazingly introspective. Many Advisors do a pitch and ask for information. The first question ALWAYS needs to be, "what would you like to get out of our conversation today?" This question creates direct alignment. Below are some other power phrases that you can plan around with. They are helpfully paired up with their more passive version so you can see the difference in how words can play a role in either paying dividends or a tax in your pursuit of trust.

Your first interview needs to unfold your process in a way that clients can feel and visualise the next steps. How long will it take, what will cost, how do you create your proposal? How will it address their needs and concerns and what about after? When do regular reviews happen, how often do you meet? If clients begin to ask you any of these questions you are not in demonstrating an interview that has strong leadership.

All of this needs to come from you in an unsolicited and confident manner. Clients want their hand held, to be told what to expect and where the turns are in the path.

In the same vein, if you can verbally construct a visual framework of your process without them needing to ask about all of the steps and hoops they need to jump through with you, your leadership will demonstrate that you are thinking of them. Alternatively, if you are focussed on the features and benefits of you or your practice in your conversation, it shows little empathy for your audience.

Telling them in a confidently understandable way creates a space where no doubt can creep in. You want them saying to themselves as they walk out your door: "Wow, she was brilliant, well spoken and knows her stuff." Your polish is your organised thoughts being presented in a powerfully exact way that puts their needs first over your ego.

Incorporating Power phrases over and over again is a systematic way to achieve this. You will notice that each of the following power phrases is a small shift from its passive counterpart. These little variations in language will produce significant gains in your trust bank. They also lend themselves to establishing a substantial amount of rapport.

Passive:	I'd like to tell you a little bit about my company and me.
Powerful:	Your story seems unique, you'll love the values that our firm is founded on.
Passive:	Which option makes the most sense for you?
Powerful:	Making a decision is an important step, many of clients sleep well at night knowing option two is working for them. Which option feels right for the both of you?
Passive:	Is this something you'd like to start today?
Powerful:	Starting today will remove the problems you mentioned earlier, we have most of the paperwork ready for you to review right now.
Passive:	I will follow-up with you once everything is moved over.
Powerful:	We will arrange for a smooth transition, after which we will be able to review everything together to ensure a solid start.

Passive: Whom do you know that might need a review of their estate?

Powerful: Since we started this relationship, I've really valued your commitment to the process, and we can see together that we have been able to improve your position. I'd be grateful to be able to create this same experience for those you respect. Which colleague do you feel could benefit from a relationship like this?

Passive: The reason for the call is you were referred to me by Joe.

Powerful: We have a mutual friend, Joe – did Joe mention I was calling? Oh, great! *(yes or no, response is the same)* last week he implemented a tax strategy that is going to help his business, and when we were done, he asked that I connect with you because he felt you'd be interested in learning more about how this same strategy might be able to help your business.

Passive:	The way that I work is either on commission or a flat fee, it depends on your total portfolio size.
Powerful:	My clients feel my pricing is fair, they have felt that having options has allowed them to decide what's best for them, I am sure you will find it the same. Shall we go over those options together now?
Passive:	I will send you a copy of your documents later this evening via email.
Powerful:	Once we process the application, I will send you a copy of your documents. Is email OK or shall I drop off the hard copies at your office in the morning?
Passive:	I don't recommend index funds because generally their performance isn't as good as managed funds.
Powerful:	Like you, I appreciate not spending more on fees than necessary. I trust though, given a choice to decide, you would want to have the world's best professional money managers working on your portfolio?

Passive: I have been in the business for 15 years and had my CFP designation.

Powerful: My clients have enjoyed partnering with me for over 15 years, and you'll feel confident that I continually educate myself professionally to the highest standards.

Passive: I help families become financially secure.

Powerful: My practice serves busy professional families who want to take the risk out of their retirement.

Passive: Thank you for referring me to Joe.

Powerful: Your referral to Joe meant a lot to me Ted, thank-you. I appreciate you thinking of me.

The Proposal Building Process

<u>Presenting</u>

Introducing the plan must be a story that was jointly written by you and your client. You would be encouraged to half-bake the proposal and then meet with your client again to bring them into the fold before presenting the final version. Vet some ideas, scenarios, strategies in that session with them. This will give you some great data points on their thinking and where they are at and not at.

This joint collaboration will give you access to their thoughts, opinions, feelings and added body language that would otherwise be reserved for the final presentation. Consider this your beta-test. You can collaboratively test a few theories out with them, and on the flip side, they see you in action, feel a part of your trusted process and receive a different experience from your competition. In the end, the close is just natural.

<u>Follow-up</u>

You have likely heard the phrase it's all about the follow-up. I remember the time I purchased my first condo. I was referred to a Real Estate Agent and never received anything from her once the deal was over. Nothing. Until Christmas, a card arrived. It was trashed immediately. All it did was remind me that she did not value my business.

A trusted follow-up realigns your promise and commitment

with your client and genuinely thanks them for choosing to work with you. After all, they do have a choice, and they chose you. My second condo, my Agent gave me a limited edition bottle of champagne she had wrapped up in my favourite colour (not her firm's colours). Classy!

Sending an email is just garbage. Do not ever send a Thank-you email and please does not take on this practice. The best approach is to do this in person, shake a hand, give a hug. Short of that, send them a gift with a custom USB and a personalised video message on it. For a big wow, send cupcakes the office of your clients who refer you business. Include a little thank-you card saying:

"Diane, thanks for sharing me with your friends, now it's my turn. Appreciate the introduction to Robert. Enthusiastically, Ty"

Now those cupcakes are going to go around, and you will be the coolest Advisor in town. Do not have a stack of business cards included in the delivery as that would diminish the value you created and the focus would be taken away from the gift and placed on you getting more business. The intention is to wow her and create an emotional connection. Keeping it subtle wins every time.

Gratitude is so important in life, not just in business and not just every time someone does business with you or sends you some new. sendoutcards.com is a great tool to help me express your gratitude. Go ahead and send yourself a free thank-you: www.sendoutcards.com/tryme

Every year, at a random time; send your entire client list a thank-you card. The front of the card may have a picture of you doing something epic or having fun family time. It doesn't need your company logo, and it's genuine. The message is something similar to this:

"Thank-you for choosing to work with me. It's because of our relationship that I am able to spend time with my family over the holidays in Mexico. My nephew learned to swim and seeing that was priceless. It is moments like this that make me pause and reflect on all those that help me and allow me to serve with grace. Appreciate you. Sending my best wishes to you and your family."

Each card is done in your handwriting if you have it scanned it and is personalised for every client. Do this today. The energy you give out will be returned tenfold.

Service Communications

The number of touch points you have with your clients will depend on your segmentation strategy and amount of value you bring to each of those groups. What information your share and the tone in which you share it will have an effect as well.

Rob, a Mortgage Broker, sent out monthly newsletters for years with little traction. The newsletter had the current rates and some local real estate news in them, and his click-open rate was miserable. Sure, he was informing, but he wasn't adding value. He then changed his format and each month he shared 1 personal item, 1 mortgage-related item and 1 fun event for families to check out in the city. His market was mainly young families. His personal item was often a picture of him and his kids doing fun things.

These two small shifts of adding value and creating intimacy by letting people know about his life took his often unopened newsletter, to a newsletter that was being shared and routinely engaged with. He credits a 32% increase in business from these changes. Do you have an email list that you could add value to?

The 5 Step Summary

Trust is not a checklist. When we think of trust and being trustworthy, the best comparison is analogizing it to a Bank. The things we do or don't do, either pay a trust dividend or a trust tax. Same with what we say or don't say, what pictures we use in our marketing, what comments we make on social media. We don't do things to earn trust, we need to be Trust in its pure form, and we can achieve that by having higher standards. Stricter standards for us, our team and in our clients.

It can start with how you prime your day and tend to your physical and mental game. Rise up and begin a new routine. Whatever you (decide to) focus on grows. Want more XYZ, focus on XYZ instead of 123

By getting to trust yourself first and use the champion voice in your head, your game is taken to a new level. This will radiate to your external world, and more of what you want will abundantly appear before you. This abundance perpetuates itself, and your Lure Factor burns with attractiveness.

By deploying emotionally intelligent sales and prospecting practices, you will create a magnetic-like level of aligned trust, and the effect will be that people want to share you often and always. Remember, as a business, your job is to add value, so continually innovate the ways in which you add value. Marketing is educating, you can increase your value inside your marketing by educating the client and prospect more at each stage within your processes. This authentic exchange comes from you being Trust, and not you selling your products, services, firm or designations.

Aligning your marketing and processes towards the core needs of humans (safety, security, family, community, etc.) is the pull you are looking for. That is the Lure Factor. The Lure Factor will radiate more for you the moment you raise your standards and commitment to being Trust in all that you do.

Bonus Chapter!

Trust Your Health - Raising Your Physical and Emotional Vitality

"How do you build trust? Trust is earned when everyone's interests are considered and respected. Communication is the key to doing this." -Sheri Levit

The energy created within you affects your emotions and your ability to make meaningful, effective decisions that are strategically smart. The more whole you are, the more attractive you become. Your energy continuously impacts your practice.

This chapter will offer you some fundamental hacks that will help you get into a state of remarkable attractiveness and sustained radiated energy that others will be magnetically drawn toward.

This section of the book will give you access to building a foundation that everything else can grow from. Without this foundation, the rest is pointless. Being healthy provides you with the daily stamina, charismatic energy, turbo cognition and glow that can compound the efforts in all areas of your life and business. If you are the type that when asked about what you want to achieve and the first thing that comes out of your mouth is more business, then this is for you.

Gerry Adair had tremendous external professional success. Internally, sadly there was a disconnect for sure. I remember lying with her on her bed about 3 months before she passed. She was terribly sick at that point. We were going through old photo albums and just talking. We had never done that before. I was 35. She occurred to me as someone who had nothing to contribute personally. Topics to discuss were always business related. It never ended with her; business was always on. In the middle of us connecting for what was really the first time in my life, she broke down.

Gerry was beyond committed to her business and serving her clients; some might say she was the definition of a workaholic. At that moment she released some energy that had her questioning "was it all worth it?" In all of my 35 years, she went on 3 vacations. Mazatlan, Hong Kong and a Vegas Re/Max conference. She worked weekends and never took time off unless she was sick, which you could imagine was often given the rate of her intensity. Her diet consisted of 2 packs of cigarettes a day, peanut butter sandwiches and whatever could be mustered up quickly.

Do not have the same regret she had in her final days. Questioning if it was all worth it is not a fulfilled life. Having the vitality, health, energy and spiritual awareness has got to be the centre point in all you do. If getting or staying healthy is something you feel you <u>should</u> do, you need to turn that should into a <u>must</u>.

You must maintain your health, as it will give you the creativity, stamina, endurance, outer glow, access to charisma and an attractive amount of abundance. Our body is a circuit board and chemistry set combined. That means you have the capacity within you to program it for high performance.

A straightforward and quick way to see if there are any blown fuses in your circuit board is to test your PH balance. If you have not peed on a PH strip, you might be in shock. The acidic body is where illness begins to set in. Nice things like yeast and bacteria thrive in an acidic body. Inflammation begins, and then chronic symptoms robbing you from all of your greatness start to grip over your physical body.

Acidosis & Alkalinity

Your body reacts to this acid by pulling minerals from your bones and other organs to help neutralise the environment. The process is slow, and over time these deficiencies add up to things like osteoporosis. Some signs that you are creating an acidic environment are low energy, cavities, sore gums, weight gain, obesity, diabetes, yeast production, poor vision, bladder and kidney infections. These are just a few and as you can see it is no party.

Foods that create an acidic base are meats, dairy, processed foods, sugar, coffee, soda. To help dimish these acidic effects, a consideration for you would be to eat meat no more than once a day. Look for vegetarian options and add leafy greens to every meal. Spinach and kale are great in omelettes as well as shakes and smoothies. Soda just needs to never be bought, and stevia is an awesome replacement for sugar. 1 cup of coffee a day is sufficient, just be wary of the caffeine and the crap you put it in like cream and refined sugar. Lemon is a great neutralizer so add a slice to each of your 8 cups a day and maybe even some Greens supplements and other adaptogens. We will explore more about adaptogens shortly. Green juices are excellent to start you off with creating alkalinity.

Masterful Mornings

When I was professional baseball umpire in MiLB, my routines were my success. Any success I had on the field that night was already achieved before I even walked out onto the field. I followed a highly regimented routine of visualisation, hydration and stretching to put myself in a position to spend 3 hours in a state of continual focus. That same regime has transferred to life outside of baseball.

Mornings are where your life is put into motion. Your day is made in the morning. Your life is made in the morning. Whatever routines you create for yourself and execute, will determine the capacity by how your day will unfold for you and whether or not you fulfill your dreams and live your purpose out.

My morning routine involves drinking a glass of water immediately after I wake up. I do my priming exercises I learned from Tony Robbins which includes diaphragmatic breathing, stretching and visualisation. I visualise what I am grateful for in that moment. It might be my dog putting her head on my lap the night before to being able to wake up to a beautiful partner, or that I have a presentation that day. I do not have a filter; I just get deeply connected. The breathing is important as it gets a significant amount of oxygen into my blood, the feeling is an awakening like no other.

This technique is a very simple form of meditation, which I return to later in the day around 2 pm. Simple breathing and focussing on gratitude. It takes me 10 minutes and keeps me connected and gives my brain a chance to focus on something else. I can be anywhere and do this. Then I hit the gym for resistance, high-intensity training or do cardio depending on where that fits into the schedule of things. However, back to the morning routine.

After my cold shower (gets the circulation going) then I have what I call my Green Supreme alkaline water which is filtered water, Greens and Ionix Supreme both from Isagenix. It is an ideal blend of super green foods, organics and few other things like CoQ10 for cardiovascular health and. The Ionix is an adaptogenic blend that helps my cells perform at their best and combat any stress that I might encounter during the day. What I am doing is priming my day to deliberately put me in the best position to align with my purpose, manage my emotions and set the intention for the day all the while experience gratitude.

Essential Oils

My priming does not stop there, though, I go into my office and rather than diving into the email I diffuse essential oils and not any essential oils. My blends are pure and include names like Determination, Active and Pure Joy. Depending on my intention for the day is how I decide which combination to use.

Diffusers disperse essential oils as a fine vapour throughout the air so they can be absorbed gently into your body through your respiratory system. The aroma can prompt your nervous system to transmit signals to the limbic system in the brain. This is the same part of the brain that houses your emotion and memory. The brain may respond by initiating various physiological functions, such as a release of hormones, relief from pain, or a positive boost in mood.

For 15 to 20 minutes with my music going and oils being diffused, I review my areas of improvement and what actions I had planned for myself the night before. This gets me focussed on what's important for that day; everything is aligned to these outcomes. Having an "ultimate question" that you answer each day will also gibe you an intentional ability to achieve a great outcome.

For me, my ultimate question is "who can I connect with right now that I can help their broad audience."

To kick all of this up a notch I listen to music that gives me goosebumps, even right this right now I have music in my ears that are giving me the tingles. I am so connected to this routine each day that I live for it. The energy I create, the gratitude I feel, and alignment with my purpose is so tight that I love how my days get going.

Priming will give you access to a new level of creation that you never knew was possible. Challenge yourself to do it for 2 weeks and see what it can do for you. Use this process to jump into your day, instead of getting immersed in email and reacting to whatever the world could be throwing at you. By 10:30 AM each day you will have aligned your energy, body and mind to a positive force that serves you, so you may serve others more brilliantly.

How goes your morning routine, how goes your day.

Ty's Morning Routine

- Drink a glass of filtered water
- Stretch your legs and back
- Deep breathing exercises with gratitude and action visioning
- Crank that music get pumped feel the day come into you
- Drink 1 glass of filtered water with Isagenix Greens and Ionix Supreme, along with your vitamins and telomere support supplements
- Quickly review your top 5 things to accomplish that day, see it and feel it unfolding for you exactly as you want it to.
- Eat high fat, high protein, low carb breakfast
- Have your shower, finish with a LONG COLD rinse to get the blood moving
- Kiss your spouse, high five your kids and tell your dog they are awesome…your day is going to rock!
- Listen to some inspirational, motivational audio on route to the office for 10-15 minutes.

This is my routine, I like to do my fitness in the afternoon around 3 or 4 pm. Modify this as you need to, but this gives you the framework to create an unleashed day.

Adaptogens

Like oils, adaptogens are another little hack that helps to maintain your mood and cellular function. Adaptogens were further popularised by Soviet Scientists looking for an edge they could provide their Olympic athletes back in the 1960's.

Essentially they are a certain small class of herbs that aid in homoeostasis. You likely remember homoeostasis from you high school science classes. The herbs with adaptogenic properties seem to support the body in creating stability at the cellular level. Think of them as performing a mitochondrial tune-up. Like any non-pharma product, there are claims that it is just hype. Many of these herbs have been used for centuries in Ayurvedic treatments and traditional Chinese medicine practices.

The modern definition for adaptogens is: "new class of metabolic regulators (of a natural origin) which increase the ability of an organism to adapt to environmental factors and to avoid damage from such factors."

The list here is believed to qualify based on the above definition:

- American Ginseng (*Panax quinquefolius*), root
- Ashwagandha (*Withania somnifera*), root
- Asian Ginseng (*Panax ginseng*), root
- Cordyceps (*Cordyceps sinensis*), mushroom/mycelium
- Dang Shen (*Codonopsis pilosula, C. tangshen*), root
- Eleuthero (*Eleutherococcus senticosus*), root/stem bark
- Green Chirayta (*Andrographis paniculata*), leaves
- Guduchi (*Tinospora cordifolia*), root/stem
- Holy Basil (*Ocimum sanctum, O. gratissimum*), herb
- Jiaogulan (*Gynostemma pentaphyllum*), herb

- Licorice (*Glycyrrhiza glabra, G. uralensis*), root
- Reishi (*Ganoderma ludicum*), mushroom/mycelium
- Rhaponticum (*Rhaponticum carthamoides*), root
- Rhodiola (*Rhodiola rosea*), root
- Schisandra (*Schisandra chinensis*), fruit/seed
- Siberian Ginseng (*Eleutherococcus Senticosus*), root,
- Shilajit (*Asphaltum bitumen*), pitch

Each of these claims to have their personal benefit from stress reduction, aiding in sleep, supporting liver function and giving natural energy. A few to highlight are Ashwagandha, Rhodiola and Eleuthero.

Remember, like any vitamin or a new diet, you would be encouraged to speak with your Dr., Herbalist, Registered Dietician, Traditional Chinese Medicine Dr. or a Dr of Naturopathy before beginning a regime of any of these.

Ashwagandha is a member of the nightshade family and is one of the most important herbs in Ayurvedic medicine. A few of the things it seems to help with are: help combat the effects of stress, improve memory and reaction times, reduces anxiety and depression, stabilises blood sugar and helps with calming inflammation.

Rhodiola is often called golden root in western cultures. A 2002 review in *HerbalGram*, the journal of the American Botanical Council, reported that numerous studies of Rhodiola in both humans and animals have indicated that it helps prevent fatigue, stress, and the damaging effects of oxygen deprivation. Evidence also suggests that it acts as an antioxidant and enhances immune system function.

Eleuthero is sometimes called Siberian Ginseng is promoted as having a broad range of health benefits, including boosting mental performance and making chemotherapy more effective; such claims are, however, not supported by Western medical evidence

Personally, I can say that since I have added adaptogens to my daily arsenal, I seem to have stronger mental clarity without the need for caffeine. More importantly, my moods are level, and I don't have the regular 3 pm slump in energy. My suggestion is to find a blend that works for you and see if there is any benefit.

Isagenix produces a mixture for cellular cleansing called Cleanse For Life and another combination for daily energy and stress management called Ionix Supreme.

Intermittent Fasting

If you have ever used a hair dryer only to have it automatically shut off because it got too hot, you know the acrid smell the heating coil gives off. Your body is no different. The overheating of the hair dryer is the same as the inflammation that goes on the body. If you use the cool setting on the hair dryer that thing will stay on for hours and so too will your body when it has the absence of disease.

Intermittent fasting is not a new concept but it is getting more attention as more science around it comes out. Diet's don't work. Intermittent fasting is not a diet. You fast every night in your sleep. Consider the word breakfast. It literally means to break the fast.

Imagine this; likely you eat every 3 of 4 hours every day of your life for as long you live. That means in this concept, your cells and digestive system are always on, always working to burn the food that just came in as opposed to burning the fat off of your body. Like any machine, they need to be turned off once and while for maintenance, repair and rest. Sleeping offers some respite, but intermittent fasting allows for even greater recovery, according to the research.

Every time you eat you produce insulin. The insulin helps to store extra energy as either sugar or fat in your liver. Once the liver is full, the greater excess is pushed out into other fat cells in your body. The reverse is true when you are not eating. Ideally, what you want to achieve is a slow burn. Like a caveman-torch with T-Rex lard as the fuel, versus a quick flame burn like taking a lighter to sugar.

The former creates acid and doesn't allow other fats to be burned instead. So when you eat fast burning foods (high glycemic), you aren't burning fat. You are burning off the sugar and causing cellular toxicity. When you eat slow burning foods grains, nuts, seeds, vegetables you are allowing for a greater capacity of fat to be burned. When you fast, you allow the largest production of fats to be burned, creating little or no toxicity. This process will allow you to achieve greater mental clarity as opposed to feeling tired after eating refined sugars and processed foods.

The thinking behind intermittent fasting is you allow your cells to have a chance to rest, repair, release waste and toxins all the while getting them ready to receive proper nutrition. By allowing your body more opportunity to burn fat you can create the potential for a leaner body and a more efficient digestive system. This is key, doesn't make sense to fast and then eat a hot dog and Coke.

Many claims to have achieved quicker fat loss and better health by deliberately skipping meals and sometimes going entire days without eating. Dr John M Berardi says Intermittent fasting can be helpful for in-shape people who want to really get lean without following traditional bodybuilding diets, or for anyone who needs to learn the difference between body hunger and mental hunger.

Personally, I fast 2-4 days a month and have experienced a leaner body, greater mental clarity and more explosive power in the gym. This combined with a steady diet of organic superfoods seems to work for me, and I have a whole community of people that it appears to work for as well. I test my blood every 6 months and have seen no deficiency or ill effect since taking this system on. Again, it's not a diet it's a pattern of eating.

Some common misconceptions about intermittent fasting are that it will burn muscle. It doesn't matter because when we fast we break down glycogen to burn glucose. You'd have to be in a severe dying of starvation mode before your body decides to start eating itself away. Another one is, isn't fasting the same as limiting calories? While it's true that you have fewer calories when fasting due to the nature of it, it's not the same as a calories restricted diets that have you focused on <u>what to eat</u> whereas fasting is about <u>when to eat</u>.

There are several patterns and systems that you could adopt into your daily life. A simple google search can lead you to those, so I won't exhaust them here. The intention is to bring this hack to the forefront of your mind so you can consider exploring it further. It certainly has given many the edge to perform better.

Thank-you for reading. If you made it this far, I must have written some decent stuff? Or your just super committed! The fact that you laid out your own money and took your valuable time to learn more about what I call the Lure Factor means a lot.

It's an area I am passionate about as I see so many Advisors that could have more, be more, help more, serve more at the level they could easily reach.

My promise to you is when you partner with me on this and raise your standards ever so slightly, and commit daily to rising and claiming your day, you will get what you came looking for when you purchased this book.

Be sure to get your bonus material at:

    www.tylerhoffman.ca/lurefactorbonus

Get the adaptogenic solutions mentioned in this book:

    www.gameplanfitness.ca

Get your TrustPro Score to see how trusted you are perceived to be:

    www.canyoutrustme.ca
    (use discount code TY15DD to get $15 off)

Uncover where you are unintentionally misstepping in the trust building process with your clients and team members.

    www.trustedpractice.ca

LURE FACTOR

"You may be deceived if you trust too much, but you will live in torment if you don't trust enough."

Frank Crane

References

https://en.wikipedia.org/wiki/Adaptogen http://www.greenmedinfo.com/ Panossian, A.; Wikman, G.; Wagner, H. (October 1999)

http://www.drweil.com/ Ades TB, ed. (2009).

"Eleuthero". *American Cancer Society Complete Guide to Complementary and Alternative Cancer Therapies* (2nd ed.). American Cancer Society. pp. 337–339. ISBN 9780944235713.

http://www.precisionnutrition.com/intermittent-fasting

Dr Jason Fung https://www.dietdoctor.com/intermittent-fasting

Steven Kotler http://time.com/56809/the-science-of-peak-human-performance

https://www.ncbi.nlm.nih.gov/pubmed/15931222

Christie Wilcox http://blogs.discovermagazine.com/science-sushi/2014/03/31/trust-trust-hormone-oxytocin-can-increase-deceit/

Paul Zak as quoted by https://www.theguardian.com/science/2011/aug/21/oxytocin-zak-neuroscience-trust-hormone?INTCMP=SRCH

Human abilities: emotional intelligence. Mayer JD, Roberts RD, Barsade SG Annu Rev Psychol. 2008; 59():507-36

http://trustedadvisor.com/why-trust-matters/understanding-trust/the-trust-quotient-and-the-science-behind-it

Check out Tyler's first book!
www.deliberatewealth.com

ABOUT THE AUTHOR

Tyler Hoffman grew up in Qualicum Beach, on Vancouver Island in British Columbia with a younger brother and a passion for baseball and umpiring. After graduating from Vancouver Island University from Recreation Administration, he attended the Academy of Professional Umpiring and went on to receive a contract in MiLB as a Professional Umpire.

After 5 years and reaching the AA level Tyler decided that life on the road was not for him and went into the financial services industry where he had a diverse career. This led him to write his first book: Deliberate Wealth.

Selling his practice in 2015, he went on to become a founding franchise partner with Shack Shine. In 2017 Tyler realigned his passion for speaking, training and writing and loves seeing the impact this brings to audiences around the world.

Tyler lives in Vancouver with his husband Sean and Jack Russell Terrier, Riley.

Trust Building Tune-up Worksheets

Trust Tax & Trust Dividends

5 Practice Management Trust Taxes

1. Client turnover
2. Redundant communication
3. Not following through
4. Weak recommendations
5. Disengagement

5 Practice Management Trust Dividends

1. Clever innovation
2. Increased added value
3. Timely execution
4. Accelerated loyalty
5. Heightened collaboration

What 3 trust taxes do you see showing up for you right now?

1. _____

2. _____

3. _____

Think about how they are inhibiting your business right now. What about your future?

What will you do to eradicate your practice from these costly trust taxes?

What trust dividends do you see happening for you?

How can you amplify these for an even greater ROI on Trust?

Accelerating Trust

- Watch your agenda, what's your motivation, how will it be perceived?
- Take a stand, share your declaration and vision
- Keep your word, honour yourself
- Own the results take responsibility
- Be vulnerable, demonstrate intimacy by being open
- Lead with your strengths

Capabilities:

- ➤ Do you have the skills and expertise to truly deliver for those you serve?
- ➤ If no, what resources do you need? How can you become more resourceful?

Character:

- ➤ Is your integrity in alignment?
- ➤ Find three relationships that you need to restore integrity and restore it by acknowledging your impact and being out of alignment and what you see possible for the relationship moving forward.

Trust Mantra

- ➤ I can be trusted because…..
- ➤ My practice can be trusted because…
- ➤ My friends can count on me knowing that…
- ➤ My family knows that I am..
- ➤ I trust myself because…

Trusted Conversation Planning

- ➢ Share your expected outcome
- ➢ Describe the current situation concisely, without emotive language, sticking to the facts
- ➢ Declare your possibility, what you see possible for each party, create a win for both

Limiting Beliefs

What are your top 3 limiting beliefs about your practice or organisation right now?

Example: My clients aren't interested in giving me referrals

1._____

2._____

3._____

How have these limiting beliefs impacted you positively?

1._____

2._____

3._____

How have these limiting beliefs impacted you negatively?

1._____

2._____

3._____

Are these beliefs true? Do you know the to be true with all your certainty? If it isn't 100% true then what's possible in its place?

1._____

2._____

3._____

What can you do right now to take massive action to dispel these limiting beliefs and move yourself forward?

1._____

2._____

3._____

Ideal Clients

What type of clients do you love serving?

Do you have these types of clients in your practice right now? If so, list them:

1._____

2._____

3._____

What can you do today to add massive value to their life and your relationship with them?

What kind of clients would you rather never have to serve again?

Do you have these types of clients in your practice right now? If so, list them:

1._____

2._____

3._____

Now fire them! Seriously. If they are not giving you the energy you need and want, find another Advisor to sell them to or gift to. If you have many these types of clients, perhaps it's an excellent time to bring in a Jr. Advisor as part of a segmentation or practice optimisation strategy.

Create a profile of your ideal client:

1. What's their age range?
2. Average Income
3. Portfolio size, or annual billings?
4. Married, kids, grandkids?
5. Is there a general industry they work in?
6. What's their biggest challenge or pain point?
7. How do they seek significance?
8. Where do they like variety?
9. How can you offer certainty or peace of mind?
10. What do they read?
11. What social media platforms do they use?
12. Do they participate in groups and forums online?

Are you reaching them 100% based on your sketch of them? What can you do this week to get in front of them more, in a way that adds value for them?

Creating Your Leadership Platform

Decide on choosing Facebook or LinkedIn to build your leadership platform on. What will the name of your platform be?

Who will you attract?

How will you add value to them? What do they get by joining?

Identify 6 "guests" that you could introduce your group to virtually, that if added, could raise your credibility and add massive value to the group.

Outline 4 articles based on your ideal client sketch that will resonate with your audience. List the juicy titles here:

1. _____

2. _____

3. _____

4. _____

Find 5 {trusted} news sources/blogs that can help you share content with your group. Think Magazines, newspapers, journals and other trusted leaders – perhaps your 6 guests above have content that is shareable?

1. _____

2. _____

3. _____

4. _____

➢ Block 30 minutes in your calendar every day, Monday through Friday so you can manage and nurture this group along. Your consistency and follow-up will be crucial for its' success.

➢ Connect with 3 members in this group each Friday directly either by phone or email to learn about the most interesting thing they are working on and what their challenges are. Take your online relationship offline and continue adding value. Block 1 hour for this.

Adding Value

What are 5 things you can do with or for your clients that will add value to them?

1._____

2._____

3._____

4._____

5._____

What do you need to do to see this though and make it happen?

1._____

2._____

3._____

4._____

When will you do this by?

If you implement all 4, what will be the outcome for them?

If you stayed consistent in doing these 4 things, in 3 years what does the future look like?

What will be the outcome for you?

If you don't implement these, what will be the outcome for them?

What will be the outcome for you?

Client Service

Start a client advisory group from a broad cross-section of clients. Meet with them every 6 months over lunch or dinner as a group and learn from them. What do they like, not like, need and not need from you? This insight will be transformational.

Who will you invite:

1. _____
2. _____
3. _____
4. _____
5. _____

When will your first meeting be?

Review all the touch points you have with your clients. What can you do in each of those to elevate the experience so that you move, touch and inspire them?

What do you have to stop doing?

How can you engage your clients more on social media?

Niche Builder Strategy: List 3 things you are passionate about or enjoy doing and give them a score of 1, 2 or 3. 3 being the thing you are the most passionate about.

1._____Score:___

2._____Score:___

3._____ Score:___

Now rate them again using the same scale. This time rate them based on the number of contacts you feel you have for each.

1._____Score:___

2._____Score:___

3._____ Score:___

Now score them each on how you feel they are as a viable market, that there is a need for what you have.

1._____Score:___

2._____Score:___

3._____ Score:___

Add them up and the 1 with the top score is a potential niche market for you!

Tyler Hoffman

-end-

Made in the USA
Columbia, SC
08 June 2017